P9-CBQ-298

Sports and Activities

Let's Ride Bikes!

by Carol K. Lindeen

Consulting Editor: Gail Saunders-Smith, PhD

Consultant: Kymm Ballard
Physical Education, Athletics, and Sports Medicine Consultant
North Carolina Department of Public Instruction

Capstone press

Mankato, Minnesota

Pebble Plus is published by Capstone Press,
151 Good Counsel Drive, P.O. Box 669, Mankato, Minnesota 56002.
www.capstonepress.com

1 2 3 4 5 6 11 10 09 08 07 06

Library of Congress Cataloging-in-Publication Data
Lindeen, Carol K., 1976–
Let's ride bikes / by Carol K. Lindeen.
    p. cm. — (Pebble plus. Sports and activities)
    Includes bibliographical references and index.
    ISBN-13: 978-0-7368-5364-4 (hardcover)
    ISBN-10: 0-7368-5364-2 (hardcover)
    1. Cycling—Juvenile literature. I. Title. II. Series.
GV1043.5.L55 2006
796.6—dc22   2005017934

Summary: Simple text and photographs present the skills, equipment, and safety concerns of biking.

Editorial Credits
Heather Adamson, editor; Kia Adams, designer; Kelly Garvin, photo researcher

Photo Credits
All images Capstone Press/Karon Dubke except page 9, Corbis/David Stoeklein and
    page 21, Getty images/Jim Cummins.

Note to Parents and Teachers

The Sports and Activities set supports national physical education standards related
to recognizing movement forms and exhibiting a physically active lifestyle. This book
describes and illustrates riding bikes. The images support early readers in understanding
the text. The repetition of words and phrases helps early readers learn new words.
This book also introduces early readers to subject-specific vocabulary words, which are
defined in the Glossary section. Early readers may need assistance to read some words
and to use the Table of Contents, Glossary, Read More, Internet Sites, and Index sections
of the book.

Table of Contents

Riding Bikes

Pedal fast! Pedal slow.

It is fun to ride bikes

with friends.

Bikes roll best

on flat, smooth ground.

Paved paths are

easy places to ride.

Some bikes race
on dirt and grass.
Knobby tires roll fast
on the bumpy ground.

Parts and Equipment

Bikes have pedals, chains, and tires. A rider's feet push the pedals to make the bike go.

chain

pedal

tire

Training wheels help
new riders learn to balance.
Riding a bike takes
lots of practice.

Biking Safety

Traffic rules keep
bike riders safe.
Riders use hand signals
to show when they
will turn or stop.

Safe bike riders

are easy to see.

They wear bright colors

and use reflectors.

reflector

Helmets cover riders' heads.
The hard shell protects them
in crashes or falls.

Having Fun

Old or young,

biking is fun for everyone.

Let's ride bikes!

Glossary

balance—to stay upright without tipping over

path—a wide strip of pavement made especially for riding bikes, walking, running, or skating

paved—covered with a very strong, hard surface used to make sidewalks and streets

pedals—levers pushed by the feet; bicycle pedals pull the chain to make a bike's back wheel turn.

reflector—a device with a shiny surface that bounces back light; reflectors help drivers of cars see bikes.

training wheels—a pair of small wheels placed on both sides of the back wheel on a bicycle to help new bike riders learn how to balance

Read More

Eckhart, Edana. *I Can Ride a Bike.* Sports. New York: Children's Press, 2002.

Klingel, Cynthia, and Robert B. Noyed. *Biking.* Chanhassen, Minn.: Child's World, 2001.

Schaefer, Lola M. *Bicycles.* Wheels, Wings, and Water. Chicago: Heinemann, 2003.

Internet Sites

FactHound offers a safe, fun way to find Internet sites related to this book. All of the sites on FactHound have been researched by our staff.

Here's how:

1. Visit *www.facthound.com*

2. Type in this special code **0736853642** for age-appropriate sites. Or enter a search word related to this book for a more general search.

3. Click on the **Fetch It** button.

FactHound will fetch the best sites for you!

Index

Word Count: 129
Grade: 1
Early-Intervention Level: 13